A Very Beaded Christmas

46 Projects That Glitter, Twinkle & Shine

Terry Taylor

LARK BOOKS

A Division of Sterling Publishing Co., Inc.
New York / London

Editor
Larry Shea

Art Director
Megan Kirby

Assistant Editor
Mark Bloom

Art Production Assistant
Jeff Hamilton

Cover Designer
Megan Kirby

Illustrator
Orrin Lundgren

Photographer
Stewart O'Shields

Library of Congress Cataloging-in-Publication Data

Taylor, Terry, 1952-
  A very beaded Christmas : 46 projects that glitter, twinkle & shine /
Terry Taylor. -- 1st ed.
      p. cm.
  Includes index.
  ISBN 978-1-60059-393-2 (pb-pbk. : alk. paper)
  1. Christmas decorations. 2. Beadwork. I. Title.
  TT900.C4T398 2009
  745.594'12--dc22

                                    2008052580

10 9 8 7 6 5 4 3 2 1

First Edition

Published by Lark Books, A Division of
Sterling Publishing Co., Inc.
387 Park Avenue South, New York, NY 10016

© 2009, Lark Books, a Division of Sterling Publishing, Inc.

Distributed in Canada by Sterling Publishing,
c/o Canadian Manda Group, 165 Dufferin Street
Toronto, Ontario, Canada M6K 3H6

Distributed in the United Kingdom by GMC Distribution Services,
Castle Place, 166 High Street, Lewes, East Sussex, England BN7 1XU

Distributed in Australia by Capricorn Link (Australia) Pty Ltd.,
P.O. Box 704, Windsor, NSW 2756 Australia

If you have questions or comments about this book, please contact:
Lark Books
67 Broadway
Asheville, NC 28801
828-253-0467

Manufactured in China

ISBN 13: 978-1-60059-393-2

For information about custom editions, special sales, premium and corporate purchases, please
contact Sterling Special Sales Department at 800-805-5489 or specialsales@sterlingpub.com.

Inside the Book

Welcome

Looking at the title of this book, you might mutter, "Oh, ho, ho, who do they think they're kidding? I don't have time for this. The holidays are coming!" But just take a minute to thumb its pages. I dare you to resist the glitter and shimmer of anything beaded. You can't. Even staunch, black-leather modernists succumb to the lure of the Christmas season with selective touches of silver, gold, and, yes, glitter.

Nothing evokes the holiday season like the sparkle of beads. Silver-lined bugle beads of all sizes. Multi-faceted glass beads as well as tiny seed beads in endless arrays of colors and finishes. Semi-precious stones and sequins, too! And I'll bet you already have many of the materials on hand to create these projects. How do I know? Well, I'm a crafter and I've got a bead stash, too. Doesn't everyone?

You might think you're too busy to stitch on hundreds of individual beads, but not to worry. With glue guns, double-sided adhesive tape, quick-drying glue—and an occasional simple stitch—you can apply beads in a jiffy. Santa's helper tells you everything you need to know starting on page 110.

Decorate your home from the mantle to the table. A bit of ribbon and some beads will stylishly show off your new Christmas cards (page 14). The retro-style Silvery Seating Arrangement (page 28) is a sure hit for any holiday meal. Little touches to your holiday decorating—like the Iced Christmas Candles on page 26—can become stylish additions for your New Year's celebrations, too.

Wreaths and stockings are everyone's favorite Christmas icons. Busy the smaller fingers in your household with stringing plastic beads onto thin wire for a crisp, modern wreath (page 54). We've got choices in this book for handcrafted stockings, large or small, to fit every home and style.

Ah, the Christmas tree! Whether yours is evergreen, plastic, feathery, or silver, you'll find a treasury of clever ornaments to trim it right. Sit down and make aromatic bay leaf ornaments, bead-dotted felt shapes, strings of glimmering crystals—even sparkling Christmas spiders and ornaments of silvery chicken wire! Just one new ornament (or a dozen) makes your tree more special.

And let's not forget those greetings and gifts that come with the season. Use vintage Christmas photographs (yours or someone else's!) to whip up some sparkly cards (page 102) the recipients will save for years. Bead-Wrapped Gift Boxes (page 98) allow you to enclose any gift in a package that will knock their Christmas stockings off. Give jars of homemade goodies with beaded felt wraps (page 104) for a memorable presentation.

Go ahead, allow yourself to be seduced by the allure of beaded things. And may all your Christmases be beadecked and bright!

Deck the Halls

Don't just trim the tree: get into the spirit of the season by decorating your entire home with holiday cheer. Ring in the season in style with projects to turn your dining room into an unforgettable banquet hall and your living room into a Christmas wonderland.

Holiday Candle Wreaths

Here's an easy place to start. Transform your candles from ho-hum into "ho-ho-ho!" with this festive wreath that you wrap around the base of a thick candle. You can also use one to turn any candle into a great gift.

WHAT YOU NEED

Pillar candle
26-gauge wire
18-mm gold star flake beads
Pearl beads
12-mm amber star flake beads
Gold round beads

WHAT YOU DO

MEASURE around the base of your candle, adding a couple inches for good measure. Cut a piece of 26-gauge wire to length. Loop the wire around a gold star flake bead and tie in a twist.

BEAD in the following order: pearl, amber star flake, gold star flake, amber star flake, gold bead, amber star flake, gold star flake, pearl, repeat.

TWIST the wire around the starting point and tuck it into the center of the bead. Trim any excess.

Designed by
SONYA NIMRI

Christmas Card Garland

Mom used to hang Christmas cards on a string. You can do better by hanging the cards from a ribbony beaded garland. Make a new one every year to save and wrap around the tree for years to come.

Designed by
JOAN K. MORRIS

WHAT YOU NEED

24-gauge wire
6-mm red faceted plastic beads
6 x 9-mm clear pony beads
16-mm glass pearl beads
30-mm green glass leaf beads
9-mm plastic pearl beads
White organza ribbon, 1½ inches (3.8 cm) wide
White star paper clips
White thread

WHAT YOU DO

CUT an 8-foot (2.4 m) length of wire. Roll up one end.

PLACE 4 inches (10.2 cm) of beads on the wire, alternating the red and clear beads. Then string the design as shown. Repeat until you run out of large pearl and leaf beads. End with 4 inches (10.2 cm) of alternating red and clear beads. Roll up the wire end.

CUT a piece of the organza ribbon 3 yards (2.7 m) long. Tie a knot every 12 inches (30.5 cm). Tie the ribbon to one end of the beaded wire. Bend the wire over and wrap it around to create a holder for the garland.

WRAP the wire around the ribbon, knotting the ribbon in place in between the knots already there. Repeat to the end. Wrap the end as before.

CUT 11 pieces of ribbon, each 12 inches (30.5 cm) long. Place a paper clip in the center of each ribbon and tie a single knot. Place the ends of the tied ribbon together and stitch across ¼ inch (6 mm) in from the edge, then zigzag the raw edge.

TIE the ribbons onto the beaded garland every 6 inches (15.2 cm) or so, using a lark's head knot (page 120).

Berry Beaded Coasters

These coasters are perfect for a hot apple cider party with the kids or a holiday eggnog bash with the neighbors. It's the beads that make the holly decorations really stand out. They can spice up any room.

Template (page 126, leaf only)

Wool felt in white, dark green, and red

Green, red, and white beading thread

11° green, red, light blue, purple, and white seed beads

Scalloped-edged fabric scissors

Designed by
MELONY BRADLEY

CUT out two leaves from green felt using the pattern. Cut three ½-inch (1.3 cm) circles from red felt for the berries. With scalloped-edged scissors, cut two circles from white felt, 4½ inches (11.4 cm) in diameter.

THREAD a beading needle with green thread. Position a leaf on the edge of one white round. Bring the needle up from back to front through the round and the leaf. Slip green seed beads onto the needle. Stitch through the opposite end, bringing the needle from the front to the back of the round. Secure the line of beads by placing a stitch every three or four beads. Create leaf veins by sewing lines of five seed beads in the same manner. Repeat for the other leaf.

THREAD the needle with red thread. Position one berry over the leaf and sew five red seed beads in random positions. Repeat for the remaining two berries.

LAYER the white rounds together, matching the scalloped edges. Thread the needle with white thread and sew pastel (light blue, green, purple, and white) seed beads to the center of each scallop using a running stitch. When the coaster edges have completely been sewn together, knot the thread at the back to secure it.

Glittering Votive Holders

These delightfully simple votive holders add holiday cheer to any table. Stick with silver beads for an elegant look, or switch to red or green for the classic Christmas style.

WHAT YOU NEED

Glass votive holder
Rubbing alcohol
Mardi Gras beads
Clear all-purpose adhesive caulk
Masking tape, ¼ inch (6 mm) wide

Designed by
ANDREA L. STERN

WHAT YOU DO

MEASURE around a votive holder. Record the measurement and then clean each votive with rubbing alcohol. Cut a string of beads to the length you need to wrap around the votive.

RUN a bead of caulk around the bottom of a votive. Carefully press the strand of beads into the caulk. Set the votive on a covered surface and let dry.

RUN a bead of caulk around the top of the votive and press another row of beads in place. Place the votive upside down on your work surface to dry.

APPLY a line of masking tape next to each line of beads. Run a line of caulk next to each strip of masking tape, and then gently remove the masking tape. Lay a strand of beads in each line of caulk. Lay the votive on its side to dry.

SANTA'S TIP: Mardi Gras beads have a "join" where the strands are fused together to make a necklace. To get the most use out of each strand, find the join and trim your beads there. If you have a gap where the beads don't meet precisely after you wrap one strand, align all of your gaps on the same side of the votive. No one will be the wiser!

Tiny Gift Boxes

A set of decorated matchboxes makes a sweet stocking stuffer. Fill them with little candies or even beads. If you leave the matches inside, keep them out of the reach of the little ones (and we don't mean Santa's elves).

WHAT YOU NEED

Matchboxes
Masking tape
Wooden paint stirrer
Gold spray paint
Craft glue
Stiff white glittered felt
Seed beads, sequins, and decorative trims

Designed by
SUZIE MILLIONS

WHAT YOU DO

EMPTY the matchsticks from the drawers. Cover the strike plates with masking tape and slip the matchbox shells onto the paint stirrer. Spray a light coat of gold spray paint on three sides. Use the stirrer to suspend the shells so they can dry untouched. When dry, remove the masking tape.

PAINT all the surfaces of the drawers except the bottom panel. When the paint is dry, spread a thin layer of tacky craft glue on the bottom of each drawer and press in a piece of white felt as a lining.

DECORATE the boxes, gluing on beads, sequins, and trims, as shown in the project photo.

SLIDE the drawers into the shells. Add the matchsticks or whatever else you want to wrap.

Beads Are Joyful!

As you work through the projects in this book, don't forget the simple joys of working with beads. In fact, use them to create a holiday message to remind you. This project shows you how.

Designed by
MELONY BRADLEY

WHAT YOU NEED

Wooden rectangle plaque, 6 x 5 inches (15.2 x 12.7 cm)

Light green acrylic paint

20-gauge beading wire

26-gauge beading wire

Light green, topaz, and green pebble beads

Light green faceted rondelle beads

Sandpaper

Paintbrush

Drill and ⅟₃₂-inch (0.8 mm) drill bit

WHAT YOU DO

SAND the plaque and paint it.

CUT the 20-gauge wire for each letter. J: 6 inches (15.2 cm) and 10 inches (25.4 cm); O: 12 inches (30.5 cm); Y: 8 inches (20.3 cm) and 6 inches (15.2 cm). Use round-nose pliers to coil one end of each.

STRING beads as follows: a light green pebble bead, a rondelle, a topaz pebble, a green pebble, a light green pebble, and a rondelle. Continue until only 3 inches (7.6 cm) remain.

SHAPE the letters. To make the J, wrap the uncoiled end of the longer piece to the center of the shorter piece. For the O, form a circle with both coils at the top. For the Y, coil both ends of the longer piece and bend into the top of a Y. Wrap the uncoiled end of the shorter piece at the bend for the bottom.

POSITION the letters on the plaque. Mark holes on each side of the letters, about ¼ inch (6 mm) apart. Position the holes so that the letters don't slip when hung. Drill the holes. Cut a 3-inch (7.6 cm) length of 26-gauge wire for each set of holes. Secure the letters on the plaque with wire threaded through the holes. Twist the wire behind the plaque, trimming the excess.

DRILL two holes at the top corners. Cut a 12-inch (30.5 cm) length of 20-gauge wire. Thread it through the holes, coiling the ends.

O Tannenbaum Napkin Rings

These fancy napkin rings bring a sparkling touch to your holiday table. Faceted glass and crystal beads blend with gold to create an understated elegance: the perfect accent for Christmas dinner.

WHAT YOU NEED

Bracelet wire

3-inch (7.6 cm) gold eye pins

2-mm gold-plated round beads

6-mm emerald green faceted fire-polished beads

6 x 2-mm gold-plated plastic rondelles

18 x 10-mm emerald and gold Czech glass Christmas tree beads

4-mm citron faceted fire-polished beads

4-mm emerald 2AB crystal bicone beads

Designed by
ANDREA L. STERN

WHAT YOU DO

MAKE a loop at one end of the bracelet wire by bending the wire 90° about ¼ inch (6 mm) from the end, and then turning the loop. This wire is stiff, so use crimping pliers to help close the loop.

MAKE connecting bars on each eye pin as follows: a 2-mm round bead, a 6-mm fire-polished bead, a rondelle, a Christmas tree, a rondelle, a 4-mm fire-polished bead, and a 4-mm bicone bead. Bend the top wire 90° and trim to about ¼ inch (6 mm) from the end. Turn a loop.

STRING onto each of the two loops of bracelet wire: a 4-mm fire-polished bead, a 6-mm fire-polished bead, and a 4-mm fire-polished bead. String a beaded connecting bar onto the wires and slide toward the end. Repeat, making sure all trees are facing the same direction, until you have used nine connecting bars, then string a 4-mm fire-polished bead, a 6-mm fire-polished bead, and a 4-mm fire-polished bead.

BEND the wire 90° and trim to ¼ inch (6 mm), then make a loop, closing with crimping pliers.

Iced
Christmas
Candles

Silver, white, and touches of blue mimic the sheen of icicles reflecting a clear winter sky. Even if it's balmy outside, this project will set the holiday mood and bring the winter of your dreams indoors.

WHAT YOU NEED

Seed beads
Bugle beads
Heavy-duty double-sided tape

Designed by
SKIP WADE

WHAT YOU DO

CHOOSE a selection of seed and bugle beads in shade of silver, white, and blue—or choose beads in your favorite holiday color scheme. Mix all of the beads together in a shallow tray or plate.

MEASURE the circumference of your candle. Cut a length of double-sided tape to your measurement.

WRAP the tape around the candle horizontally. Remove the protective film on the outside of the tape.

ROLL the candle in the bead mixture, pressing beads into place with your fingers as needed.

SANTA'S TIP: Pillar candles are easiest to work on, but you could use the same technique with tapers: Imagine diagonal stripes of red seed beads for a traditional pepperminty look.

Silvery Seating Arrangement

There'll be no more squabbles about who sits where at your holiday dinner party when you add one of these place card holders to every setting. Make a few more than you need to seat the last-minute additions you're bound to have.

WHAT YOU NEED

Toothpicks
White foam cones
Iridescent clear glass bugle beads
6-mm round silver plastic beads
20-gauge wire
Tinsel garland
Fast-drying tacky craft glue
Hot glue gun
Cardstock

Designed by
SUZIE MILLIONS

WHAT YOU DO

STICK a toothpick deep into the top point of each cone as a handle.

POUR bugle beads onto a paper plate. Spread glue over the surface of the cone. Press it down into the bugle beads and rotate to coat. Don't force the beads on and don't worry about the cone showing through—a light application of beads is enough. Set aside to dry.

REMOVE the toothpick and brush off excess or stray beads. Attach round silver beads to the cones using hot glue, spacing them about ½ inch (1.3 cm) apart.

CUT a 5-inch (12.7 cm) length of wire. Grasp the end with needle-nose pliers and turn it one revolution to make a tight coil. Continue to turn the pliers, wrapping the remaining wire loosely around the center coil. Bend the last ¾ inch (1.9 cm) at a 90° angle to make a stem.

ARRANGE a small poof of tinsel garland around the base of each coil. Put a pea-size puddle of hot glue on the top of a cone and push the stem of a cardholder down into it, pinning the tinsel poof in the glue.

CUT cardstock into 1½ x 3-inch (3.8 x 7.6 cm) place cards. Write the name of a guest on each card and slip one into each cardholder.

Winter Lace Place Mats

Even if you never use place mats the rest of the year, try these out during the holidays to give your table a festive flair. This project uses a simple design to show off your most beautiful fabric.

WHAT YOU NEED

Nylon beading thread
Place mats
Seed beads (sizes 11°, 8°, and/or 6°)

Designed by
GEORGIE ANNE JAGGERS

WHAT YOU DO

CUT a 5-foot (1.5 m) length of beading thread. Double the thread on the needle and tie the two ends in a knot. Starting in the corner of the place mat, sew from underneath up through the right side.

STRING seed beads in any order that you like. Use a ruler along the edge of the place mat to space out the fringe evenly.

SEW back down through the top of the place mat's edge to the wrong side. Sew back up to the top of the edge. Repeat until that side of the place mat is complete, ending with the needle and thread on the reverse side.

TIE a knot at the back and trim the thread just above the knot.

Frosty Beaded Garland

You can wrap anything with this garland: trees, banisters, even candles! Use various styles and sizes of beads to create different looks, but whatever beads you use, it will look fabulous.

WHAT YOU NEED

Assorted beads ranging from seed beads to 10-mm beads

26-gauge bright wire

Designed by
SKIP WADE

WHAT YOU DO

POUR all the beads into a large bowl, mixing well with your hands.

UNROLL about 3 inches (7.6 cm) of wire and dip the wire into the bead bowl, scooping up beads and stringing on beads. Continue scooping and adding beads, unrolling the wire a few more inches after each scoop. Once you have about 3 feet (91.4 cm) of wire covered in beads, loop the wire around the last bead, being sure to leave some extra wire between the last bead and the other beads.

TWIST the wire every few inches, creating a small loop of beaded wire.

REPEAT until you've made enough garland for whatever you'd like to decorate.

Regal Table Runner

This beaded table runner makes dinner into an elegant occasion: it sets the stage for your most special crystal and china. Add a few silver bells, and your family will wonder what five-star hotel they wandered into.

WHAT YOU NEED

Store-bought or handmade table runner
Beaded ribbon trim
Sequin trim
Fabric glue

Designed by
SKIP WADE

WHAT YOU DO

MEASURE the sides and ends of the runner and cut four pieces of the beaded ribbon and sequin trims to length.

RUN a thin bead of glue along the sides and ends of the runner. Gently press the beaded ribbon onto the bead of glue. Let dry.

ADHERE the sequin ribbon on top of the beaded ribbon.

Very Merry Magnets

Santa, snowmen, Christmas trees—any image you choose will work in these holiday-themed magnets. They'll sparkle and shine wherever you place them. They'll bring a smile even to Scrooge's face.

Designed by
JOAN K. MORRIS

WHAT YOU NEED

- Assorted clip art of retro Christmas designs
- Paper punch with a 1½-inch (3.8 cm) hole (optional)
- ¾-inch (1.9 cm) letter stickers
- 1½-inch (3.8 cm) crystal clear round glass nuggets
- Glossy decoupage medium
- Pre-beaded seed bead wires in red, green, and clear
- Quick-set epoxy
- ¾-inch (1.9 cm) button magnets

WHAT YOU DO

CUT out 1½-inch (3.8 cm) circles from your chosen designs, using the paper punch or scissors. Choose the order for your lettering. Stick the letters onto the cut-out circles.

ADHERE the glass nuggets on top of the cut-out circles with the decoupage medium. Rub any bubbles off to the edge. Let dry. Trim off any excess paper around the edge of the glass nugget. Cover the back with two thin coats of decoupage medium to seal.

CUT the beaded wire to the circumference of the nugget plus 1 inch (2.5 cm). Remove the extra beads and twist the wire ends together, making a circle. Trim the excess twisted wire to ⅛ inch (3 mm).

GLUE the beads to the outside edge of the glass nugget with epoxy. Let dry. Fold the twist of wire to the back of the glass nugget; keep it in position with a dab of epoxy.

USE epoxy to attach the magnet to the center of the back of the glass nugget. Let dry.

Sparkling Snowflake Mats

Are you dreaming of a white Christmas? No matter what the weather outside, create a seasonal flurry with soft white felt and silvery sequins. Talk about a winter wonderland—now   can make one yourself.

WHAT YOU NEED

White thread

Store-bought or homemade white felt place mat

Small geometric glass beads

White snowflake-shaped sequins

Long glass beads

White round sequins

Permanent fabric glue

Designed by
SKIP WADE

WHAT YOU DO

RUN a threaded needle through the placemat from the back to the outside edge. Thread on a small glass bead, a snowflake sequin, and another small glass bead. Wrap the thread around the last bead and run it back through the other beads and the mat. Pull the thread tightly.

REPEAT around the place mat, spacing each bead/sequin group 1 to 2 inches (2.5 to 5.1 cm) apart.

APPLY a thin line of glue around the placemat, 1 inch (2.5 cm) from the edge. Glue the long beads in place, side by side around the entire diameter.

RUN a threaded needle through the place mat from the back, about 1 inch (2.5 cm) toward the center from the line of long beads. Thread on a snowflake sequin, a round sequin, and a small glass bead. Wrap the thread around the last bead and run it back through the other beads and the mat. Pull the thread tightly.

REPEAT around the place mat, spacing each bead/sequin group 1 to 2 inches (2.5 to 5.1 cm) apart.

Jolly Snowman Mirror

Decoupage medium creates the finish and pattern paper provides the color, but the festive snowman makes this small wall-hanging mirror an object of desire (and compliments). See your reflection surrounded by your handiwork.

WHAT YOU NEED

- 10-inch (25.4 cm) square, framed mirror
- White and black acrylic paint
- White textured paint
- Striped, snowflake, and winter word patterned paper
- Matte-finish decoupage medium
- Die-cut chipboard snowman, top hat, and ½-inch (1.3 cm) circles
- White pearl and black seed beads
- Ribbon
- Thick white glue
- Foam adhesive tape
- ½-inch (1.3 cm) paintbrush
- Sponge brush

WHAT YOU DO

PAINT the frame's inside and outside edges white.

CUT three pieces of paper, each 10 x 3⅓ inches (25.4 x 8.5 cm), to cover the frame. Trim as necessary to expose the mirror. Decoupage the paper to the mirror using the sponge brush, smoothing away any bubbles with your fingers. When dry, add a coat of decoupage medium to seal it.

LAYER white textured paint onto the top and edges of the chipboard snowman. Sprinkle on white seed beads and press them into the wet paint. Cover the snowman thoroughly, and then place black seed beads for the eyes. Allow it to dry completely. Cover it with a thin coat of decoupage medium to seal it.

PAINT the chipboard hat and circles black. When dry, spread a thin layer of white glue on the hat brim and cover it with black seed beads. Allow it to dry. Glue the hat and circle buttons onto the snowman.

MAKE a scarf by tying ribbon around the snowman's neck. Glue the snowman to the left side of the frame. Add foam adhesive under the hat for added support.

GLUE white seed beads to graphic elements on the paper design, such as the snowflakes in the project photo.

Designed by
CARLA SCHAUER

Miniature Mantel Trees

If you love Christmas trees, you don't want to limit yourself to just one. Here's a project that lets you add beautifully ornate trees throughout the house. Start on the mantel, and then spread the joy!

WHAT YOU NEED

- Polystyrene foam cones and block
- Dark green satin
- Green felt
- Spray adhesive
- Craft glue
- Dowel, 7-inch (17.8cm)
- Clear flexible beading wire
- Silver or gold crimp beads
- 4-mm, 6-mm, and 10-mm round crystal beads
- 4-mm and 6-mm faceted fire-polished glass beads
- 6-mm gold-cupped sequins
- Straight pins
- Gold glitter
- Flowerpots, 8 inches (20.3 cm) in diameter
- Polyester fiberfill stuffing

WHAT YOU DO

COVER each cone with the satin using spray adhesive, pressing to smooth and trimming the fabric as necessary.

PRESS the dowel 1 inch (2.5 cm) into the center of the cone bottom, and then remove it. Glue a felt circle to the cone bottom. Cut the hole open with a pair of sharp scissors.

CUT 5-inch (12.7 cm) pieces of the flexible beading wire. String one piece through a crimp bead and then back, leaving an ⅛-inch (3 mm) loop. Crimp the bead, and then string beads as shown in the photo. Use about 13 beads, with the largest bead in the center. String on another crimp bead, make another loop, and crimp the bead.

PUT a 4-mm crystal bead and a sequin on a straight pin, then catch the loops on the ends of two beaded strands. Push the pin into the cone, starting about 1½ inches (3.8 cm) from the bottom. Go around the cone, pinning through two loops each time.

MOVE up about 1½ inches (3.8 cm) for the next row, putting the first pin in the center of a drop. Continue until strands fill the cone.

CUT a 7-inch (17.8 cm) length of dowel and sand the ends. Spray it with adhesive and cover it with glitter to 1 inch (2.5 cm) from the ends.

CUT the florists' foam in half with a kitchen knife and place each half into a flowerpot. Stick one end of the dowel into the center of the foam. Apply a thin coat of glue on the other end and then slide the cone tree onto it. Fill the pot with the stuffing. Lightly spray with adhesive and sprinkle glitter on the fill.

Designed by
ANDREA L. STERN

SANTA'S TIP: Try using iridescent packing excelsior or some beads to top off the pot.

Auld Lang Signs

From Christmas to New Year's, your family and friends celebrate with clinking glasses. These wineglass markers cleverly and tastefully signal their owners. Make enough for a party.

WHAT YOU NEED

Pinch bail finding

20-mm AB finish crystal snowflake

Stainless steel memory wire,
½ inch (1.3 cm) in diameter

Assorted 3- to 6-mm beads and crystals in desired colors

Silver snowflake charms

Ribbon

Wineglasses

Designed by
CANDIE COOPER

WHAT YOU DO

CONNECT a pinch bail to the hole in the crystal snowflake using chain-nose pliers.

CHECK the length of your wineglass stem to gauge how much to stretch the memory wire coil, and gently pull each end of the coil to add length. Make a loop at one end of the coil and connect the loop to the pinch bail/crystal snowflake charm.

STRING beads randomly or in a pattern. Add a snowflake charm when you reach the middle section. Continue stringing and make a loop at the end of the coil. Connect a snowflake charm to the loop.

TIE a piece of ribbon around the top of the coil and trim ends to desired length.

Wreaths&Stockings

Nothing says Christmas like a wreath on the door and stockings hanging from the mantel. These projects give you both traditional and innovative options for those classic Yuletide symbols. Don't have a fireplace? These spectacular stockings will look great anywhere. And having just one wreath on the front door won't be enough anymore.

Pretty Poinsettia Wreath

Everyone loves poinsettias during the holidays. It's probably all those petals the color of Santa's suit. Just as Santa returns every year, so will this wreath—its flowers are crafted out of red felt.

Red felt

Green felt

Polystyrene foam wreath, 12 inches (30.5 cm) in diameter

Flat- and round-head straight pins, 2 inches (5.1 cm) long

Assortment of clear glass beads, gold filigree beads, gold seed beads, and gold sequins

Designed by
SONYA NIMRI

MEASURE and cut the red felt into 4½ x 6-inch (11.4 x 15.2 cm) pieces as needed to cover the front and sides of the wreath. Pin in place with flat-head pins at the corners, smoothing the fabric and trimming the excess.

CUT out approximately 13 green leaves measuring 3 x 3 inches (7.6 cm x 7.6 cm) at the widest point. Pin from the center top points to the wreath, cascading over the sides.

CUT out approximately 120 red petal shapes in a variety of sizes. Layer seven petals at the center point to make each flower and pin in the center with a flat-head pin. Fill in the back of the flowers with random collections of two or three petals, pinning in the middle top of the petals.

MARK the center of each poinsettia with an assortment of beads attached with round-head pins.

Santa's Favorite Stockings

Santa might be tempted to take these stockings home to surprise Mrs. Claus. Just to make sure that doesn't happen, maybe you should bead your family's initials or names onto the cuff!

WHAT YOU NEED

Template (page 125)
Fabric, ½ yard (45.7 cm)
Complementary or contrasting fabric, ½ yard (45.7 cm)
Matching thread
Assortment of e-beads or seed beads

Designed by
TERRY TAYLOR

WHAT YOU DO

PHOTOCOPY the template and enlarge as desired. Fold one piece of fabric right sides together. Pin the template to the fabric and cut out the shape.

STITCH the stocking together with a ¼-inch (6 mm) seam allowance. Turn the stocking right side out.

MEASURE the top of the stocking. Double the width of the stocking top and add ½ inch (1.3 cm) to the measurement. Decide how deep you want the cuff to be.

FOLD the second fabric right sides together. Mark a rectangle along the folded edge to the length you measured by the depth you want the cuff. Cut out the rectangle. Unfold and stitch the short sides together with a ¼-inch (6 mm) seam.

TURN the tube right side out, and then match the top and bottom edges, wrong sides together, to create a narrower tube.

TUCK the cuff into the stocking, matching the raw edges. Pin together and stitch with a ¼-inch (6 mm) seam. Turn the cuff right side out and press.

MAKE a mixture of beads and stitch them to the cuff as desired.

Bethlehem Beaded Stars

These eye-catching, easy-to-make stars are sure to impress, whether you place them on your tree, your stockings, or your wreath. Make a whole bunch and they'll light up your season.

WHAT YOU NEED

28-gauge silver wire

¾-inch (1.9 cm) round glass bead

Assortment of glass beads:
  e-beads up to ¾-inch (1.9 cm) beads

Quick-setting epoxy

Designed by
JOAN K. MORRIS

WHAT YOU DO

CUT four pieces of wire 12 inches (30.5 cm) long. Bend two in half. Holding the center of the bent wires together, wrap a straight wire around them. Spread the wire out into a star shape.

GLUE the large bead in the center of the wire star using the epoxy. Let dry.

CUT two pieces of wire 6 inches (15.2 cm) long. Run the remaining 12-inch (30.5 cm) wire and the two 6-inch (15.2 cm) wires through the center bead. Bend the ends of one of the shorter wires to the back and twist tightly together over the rest of the wires to secure them. Bend the twisted

wire flat to the bead. Bend the other short wire to the back, but leave the longer wire straight to complete the eight-pointed star.

GLUE the twisted wire to other wires to hold their position. Let dry.

PLACE beads on the wires, matching beads on the opposite wires. Experiment until you like the look. At each star point, wrap the end of the wire under with needle-nose pliers. Trim any excess wire.

USE the remaining 6-inch (15.2 cm) wire to hold the star in place.

Frozen Christmas Wreath

Tired of wreaths that wilt before the season is over? Wire and festive beads form a contemporary wreath you can use again and again.

WHAT YOU NEED

WHAT YOU NEED

22-gauge bright wire
26-gauge bright wire
Green, blue, and clear pony beads
Wire wreath frame
Silver spray paint

Designed by
SKIP WADE

WHAT YOU DO

UNROLL a length of 22-gauge wire about 6 inches (15.2 cm) long, but do not cut it. Slide on beads to fill, and wrap the wire around the last bead to secure it. Space the beads about 2 inches (5.1 cm) apart and twist the wire around each bead, securing it in place. Wrap the wire around the last bead to secure it and cut the wire. Create several more 22-gauge garlands and set aside.

REPEAT the previous step using the 26-gauge wire.

PAINT the wire wreath frame with silver spray paint and allow it to dry.

WRAP the beaded 22-gauge wires around the painted wreath frame. Some of the wire should be wrapped tightly to the frame and some loosely.

WRAP the beaded 26-gauge wires around the painted wreath frame. Most of the wire should be loosely wrapped around so that it appears to be floating.

Away in a Manger Stockings

The natural look of these stockings—gently frayed edges and soft colors—comes from using burlap as a fabric foundation. You dress it up with beads and ribbon.

WHAT YOU NEED

Templates (pages 125–127)
White, sage, and dark green burlap
Matching sewing threads
Invisible thread
Double-sided iron-on adhesive
3-mm red glass beads
12-mm yellow glass beads
16-mm square brass beads
20-mm oblong brass beads
8-mm green glass beads
Bone beads, assorted sizes
Green ribbon, ⅛ inch (3 mm) wide

Designed by
JOAN K. MORRIS

WHAT YOU DO

MAKE patterns from the templates. Cut out two stocking pieces and two cuffs from the white and sage burlap.

STAY-STITCH around each piece, ⅛ inch (3 mm) from the edge using matching sewing threads. Trim the edges evenly. Stitch on the contrasting cuffs.

FUSE the iron-on adhesive to the dark green burlap. Cut out tree and holly designs from the templates. Adhere the designs to the front of each stocking. If desired, machine stitch around the designs with a zigzag stitch.

STITCH the beads in place using the invisible thread.

CUT 10 inches (25.4 cm) of the green ribbon and fold it in half to form a loop. Place the loop at the top of the stocking and stitch it in place.

PIN a front and back stocking piece wrong sides together. Stitch the stockings together.

Beaded
Eucalyptus
Wreath

Here's a project that makes use of a wreath you already have. Dress up a plain eucalyptus wreath with beaded embellishments. Its sweet smell and festive look is sure to please you and your family.

WHAT YOU NEED

28-gauge green floral wire

1¼-inch (3.2 cm) gem-shaped plastic crystal beads

1-inch (2.5 cm) round plastic crystal beads

3-mm gold-colored beads

¾-inch (1.9 cm) faceted plastic crystal beads

10-mm round faceted iridescent glass beads

12-mm gold-colored decorative filler beads

¼-inch (6 mm) gold-colored cord

Eucalyptus wreath, 10 inches (25.4 cm) in diameter

WHAT YOU DO

CUT 30 pieces of the 28-gauge green floral wire 8 inches (20.3 cm) long.

MAKE six ornaments as follows: Run one end of one wire through one of the gem-shaped beads, wrap the short end back up to the wire, and twist together at the bead. Place an assortment of four beads on the wire.

USE the 1-inch (2.5 cm) round beads to make six more ornaments. Place a 3-mm gold bead on the end and twist. Now place the large round bead and then four assorted beads.

MAKE twelve ornaments with the ¾-inch (1.9 cm) faceted crystal beads and six with the 10-mm round iridescent beads at the bottom.

CUT an 18-inch (45.7 cm) length of gold cord and tie the raw edges together, making a circle. Tie the cord to the wreath with a lark's head knot (page 120). Attach the ornaments to the wreath by wrapping the wire around the structure or the eucalyptus stems and then around the wire at the base of the ornament.

Designed by
JOAN K. MORRIS

Stockings for the Elves

Fill these diminutive stockings with candy and hang them on your tree. Tuck a gift card inside for a one-of-kind present presentation. Hang them on your mantel for your pets (they deserve presents too!).

WHAT YOU NEED

Templates (page 125)
Quilted fabric
Lining fabric
Sewing thread
Felt beads
Assortment of seed beads and e-beads
Sequins
Metal charms
Yarn

Designed by
LINDA WILLIS

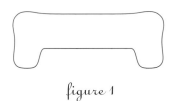

figure 1

WHAT YOU DO

PHOTOCOPY two copies of the template.

FOLD each piece of fabric in half, right sides together. Mark the template shapes on the material. Stitch the stockings along the lines, except for the marked openings. Cut them out, leaving a ¼-inch (6 mm) seam allowance.

TURN the lining material right side out. Stuff it inside the quilted stocking, lining up the seams. Stitch them together along the top using a ¼-inch (6 mm) seam allowance. Pull the lining out of the stocking and stitch the opening closed. Stuff the lining back in place. Topstitch around the top of the stocking and then fold down a 2-inch (5.1 cm) cuff (figure 1).

ADORN the felt beads. Randomly stitch seed beads to the surface, attach sequins with seed beads, or stitch on a combination of e-beads and seed beads.

SEW the felt beads to the stocking cuff. Sew into the cuff, pick up 10 seed beads, and then sew through the felt bead. Finish as described above. Optionally, sew on a row of metal charms to dangle below the cuff.

LOOSELY twist together three 18-inch (45.7 cm) strands of yarn. Machine stitch them together with a zigzag stitch. Use the yarn as you would a woven trim, stitching it to the stocking cuff. Optionally, bead a loop for hanging.

Snowy Sequin Wreath

There are natural-looking wreaths and there are spectacular-looking wreaths. Your friends and neighbors will remember this one because of the way it resembles a sparkling snowfall.

WHAT YOU NEED

Extruded polystyrene foam wreath, 6 inches (15.2 cm) in diameter

Gesso paint or white polystyrene foam paint

Flat-head straight pins

3-mm blue glass beads

10-mm silver plastic beads

¾-inch (1.9 cm) iridescent blue palette sequins

¾-inch (1.9 cm) silver palette sequins

White cord

Industrial-strength clear multipurpose adhesive

WHAT YOU DO

PAINT the foam wreath white. It may take three coats to cover. Let dry.

PIN the beads and sequins around the inside of the wreath. Place a blue 3-mm bead on a flat-head straight pin, followed by a 10-mm silver bead and a blue sequin. Alternate the blue and the silver all the way around the center.

PIN the next row of beads and sequins close to the first, lining up the same colors together. Place them a little off center from each other to start creating the spiral.

KEEP adding rows, each row a little off from the one before, until you reach a little beyond halfway to the outside back of the wreath. You will probably have six rows.

DAB a little of the adhesive with a toothpick under each sequin and press the sequin in place. Allow the adhesive to dry.

MAKE the hanger by folding a 12-inch (30.5 cm) length of white cord in half and tie a knot at the top. Attach it to the back of the wreath with straight pins.

Designed by
JOAN K. MORRIS

Oh Christmas Tree

Now it's time to focus on your tree. Whether it's real or artificial, you can find handmade projects here to make it sparkle, twinkle, or dazzle. Ornaments, garlands, and even Creeping Christmas Spiders await you. Turn the page and get busy!

Cookie Cutter Christmas

These ornaments are anything but ordinary. Using holiday cookie cutters shaped like a Christmas tree or a snowman, you craft exquisite ornaments to add a little cheer to your tinsel.

WHAT YOU NEED

Cookie cutters

28-gauge silver wire

Seed beads

Assortment of pony, bugle, and e-beads

Pre-beaded wire

Drill with small drill bit

Designed by
JOAN K. MORRIS

WHAT YOU DO

DRILL evenly spaced holes down the sides of the cookie cutters, ¼ inch (6 mm) in from the front edge. Drill a hole in the center top too.

CUT a 30-inch (76.2 cm) length of wire. Thread a seed bead. Fold the short end over the bead and twist in place. Thread the wire from the outside into the cookie cutter. The seed bead acts as a stop bead.

THREAD assorted beads onto the wire to fill up the length inside the cookie cutter. Run the wire through the opposite hole. Place a seed bead on the wire, run the wire through the next hole on the cookie cutter, and pull tightly. Continue stringing beads and weaving the wire through the holes, placing a seed bead outside each hole. At the end, twist the wire around the last seed bead and trim the excess wire.

CUT a 12-inch (30.5 cm) length of pre-beaded wire for the hanger. Remove 6 inches (15.2 cm) of beads. Twist the ends together. Run the wire through the top hole in the cookie cutter. Place a bead on the twisted wire and run the wire back out the hole. Twist all the wires together at the bottom of the beads and cut off any excess wire.

Glimmering
Crystal
Icicles

Hanging from your tree or along your mantel, these gorgeous ornaments resemble the icicles that line your roof in winter, but these icicles will warm your heart. Place them near your tree lights for maximum dazzle.

WHAT YOU NEED

Flexible beading wire

Crimp tubes

Clear seed beads

4- to 10-mm colored crystal beads

4- to 10-mm clear crystal beads

Crystal prism

WHAT YOU DO

CUT a 10-inch (25.4 cm) length of flexible beading wire for each ornament.

THREAD a crimp tube onto the wire, followed by seed beads, the crystal prism, and more seed beads. Mix in clear and colored crystal beads on other ornaments for variety.

RUN the other end of the wire through the crimp tube, positioning the tube to fit the beads tightly together. Use needle-nose pliers to flatten the crimp tube.

Designed by
GEORGIE-ANNE JAGGERS

Fun Fiber Garland

"Funky" and "over-the-top" describe this whimsical take on a traditional garland. If you have a tree filled with an eclectic collection of ornaments, this garland adds a contemporary, casual touch.

WHAT YOU NEED

Felt beads

Seed beads

Sequins

E-beads

Beading thread

Four or more novelty yarns (the more the merrier!)

Silver and copper embroidery thread

Glittery netting

Designed by
LINDA WILLIS

WHAT YOU DO

EMBELLISH your felt balls with beads in a variety of ways. Randomly stitch seed beads to their surfaces, attach sequins to the balls with seed beads, or stitch a combination of e-beads and seed beads on the balls. When you finish each bead, knot the thread, and then pull the knot up into the bead to hide it.

CUT one variety of novelty yarn into 6-inch (15.2 cm) pieces. Cut the other yarns, embroidery thread, and netting into 4-inch (10.2 cm) pieces. Bundle two or three of the shorter lengths together. Tie them together in the center with a 6-inch (15.2 cm) length of yarn. Make a lot of bundles!

CUT four different yarns into 6-foot (1.8 m) lengths. Loosely twist the yarns together and machine stitch them together using a wide zigzag stitch.

THREAD the yarn onto a large-eye needle. String the felt beads onto the yarn, spacing them evenly. Knot both ends of the yarn, leaving a tail at each end.

TIE bundles of yarn along the length of the garland using 6-inch (15.2 cm) lengths of yarn.

Festive Floating Beads

Fun bead combinations and thin wire produce ornaments that seem to float on your tree. Chicken wire, also known as metal poultry fencing, comes in large rolls, so make a lot of these.

WHAT YOU NEED

1-inch (2.5 cm) chicken wire
28-gauge silver wire
Silver square and decorative beads
Glass beads
Dangle beads
Large-hole bead, 10–12 mm
Silver cord

Designed by
JOAN K. MORRIS

WHAT YOU DO

CUT out the shape you want from the chicken wire using wire cutters. This stuff is sharp, so wear protective gloves. Snip as close as you can to the edge at the corners, then file the corners smooth. Leave the top and bottom twisted pieces ½ inch (1.3 cm) long. (If you cut too close, it will unravel.)

CUT a piece of the silver wire 8 inches (20.3 cm) long for each section of the chicken wire to be beaded. Wrap the wire around the spot you want to start the beads and twist, using needle-nose pliers if necessary. String the beads onto the wire and wrap the other end. Trim excess wire.

THREAD the large-hole bead on the bottom ½ inch (1.3 cm) of twisted wire. With needle-nose pliers, bend the twisted wire over to hold the bead in place.

CUT a piece of the silver cord 12 inches (30.5 cm) long. Fold it in half and tie a knot at the cut ends. Attach the cord to the top of the ornament using a lark's head knot (page 120).

Creeping Christmas Spiders

Face your fears the fun way! These aren't creepy spiders to frighten you; they're brightly beaded spiders to liven up your holidays. Stick them in your tree to surprise your guests ... and the Grinch.

Designed by
MELONY BRADLEY

WHAT YOU NEED

26-gauge beading wire
10-mm faceted crystal bead
6-mm pearl bead
Black pebble beads
Pastel seed beads
4-mm pearl beads
Oval beads
Crystal faceted rondelles
Crystal faceted teardrops
Silver thread

WHAT YOU DO

CUT five 6-inch (15.2 cm) lengths of wire. Bend the end of one wire around the barrel of a marker to form a loop for hanging. Twist the end around the wire to secure.

THREAD beads onto the wire in the following sequence: one 10-mm bead for the head, one 6-mm bead for the body, one black pebble bead for the eye, two pastel seed beads for the fangs, and one black pebble for the remaining eye. To form eyes and fangs, wrap the top of the wire around the fang and eye beads. Trim off excess wire.

GATHER the remaining wires for the legs by holding the wires in the middle and wrapping them around the wire between the head and body bead. Thread beads onto the legs in the following sequence: one pearl, one oval, one rondelle, one teardrop, and one pearl. To secure the beads, form a loop at the end of the leg with round-nose pliers. Repeat for the remaining seven legs. Shape legs as desired.

LOOP thread through the wire loop as the hanger.

Aromatic Star Ornaments

Did the Three Kings follow a bright star or a scented one? The secret to this project is the bay leaves. They'll provide a lovely aroma and last a long time. How many stars can say that?

WHAT YOU NEED

Fabric trim, 1 inch (2.5 cm) wide
Gold cord
Green plastic foam disk, 4 x 1 inches (10.2 x 2.5 cm)
Large bead with a large hole
12-mm or larger round glass beads
Straight pins
Gold ball-tipped pin with a large ball
Smaller gold ball-tipped pins
Bay leaves

Designed by
SUZIE MILLIONS

WHAT YOU DO

WRAP the fabric trim snugly around the foam disk and secure the ends with a straight pin.

CUT 12 inches (30.5 cm) of gold cord and double it to form a loop. Knot the ends. Pinch the top of the loop and thread the large bead over it, pulling it against the knot. Push a large ball-tipped pin through the bead and knot.

PUSH the assembled hanger into the foam disk, over the seam of the fabric trim. Angle in straight pins on both sides, through the knot and into the disk.

SORT the bay leaves into 16 whole "top-layer" leaves and 16 broken "bottom-layer" leaves for each ornament.

POSITION four bottom-layer leaves to point north, south, east, and west. Fasten each leaf in place with two straight pins. Add four more leaves between the first set.

ADD the top-layer leaves, placing them in the gaps. Pin them in place with two smaller ball-tipped pins in the leaves' center vein.

CLUSTER three smaller ball-tipped pins in the center of the ornament. Arrange another six to 10 pins around the same spot.

SLIP a round glass bead onto a pin. Stick it in the space between two top-layer leaves. Continue around the ornament. Cover the other side as well.

SANTA'S TIP: If you can't find small gold-tipped pins, stick about 100 pins into a foam disk and spray paint them yourself. If the ball-tipped pins are longer than 1 inch (2.5 cm), snip off the ends so they don't poke through.

Satin Ball Ornaments

Shiny satin and bejeweled beads make these ornaments really sparkle. Looking at them hanging from your tree, you'll get the urge either to rip open presents or rip it up on the dance floor.

WHAT YOU NEED

3-inch (7.6 cm) satin-covered polystyrene foam ball ornament

18-mm round crystal rhine-stone jewels

Pre-beaded gold seed bead wire

Super textile adhesive

Designed by
JOAN K. MORRIS

WHAT YOU DO

PLACE the satin ornament in a paper cup with the top up. Glue on the crystal rhinestone jewels with the textile adhesive, placing four evenly spaced at the top with enough room around each to add the beaded wire. Work your way down the ball, gluing the jewels around the first four. Allow it to dry completely.

MAKE bead circles by wrapping the beaded wire around a jewel. Cut the wire ½ inch (1.3 cm) longer than the circle and remove the extra beads. Use needle-nose pliers to wrap the wire so the rest of the beads don't fall off. Twist the ends together to create a circle. Trim the wire twist to ⅛ inch (3 mm). Hide the twist under the circle.

PLACE the beaded circles by dabbing glue on the wrong side of the circle and then carefully placing the circles around the jewels.

SANTA'S TIP: If you can't find pre-beaded wire, make your own using 26-gauge wire and gold seed beads.

Silent Night Stars

These stitched and stuffed star ornaments twinkle on your tree, courtesy of sparkling beads. The pure white felt helps them stand out like the Star of Bethlehem.

WHAT YOU NEED

White wool felt

Gold and silver embroidery floss

3-mm bicone crystal glass beads

4-mm gold and silver filigree balls

3-mm frosted and crystal rectangle beads

14-mm faceted glass crystal disks

4-mm flat-back pre-glued crystals

Polyester fiberfill stuffing

Pre-glued crystal applicator wand

Designed by
LORINE MASON

WHAT YOU DO

CUT stars out of the felt, sized as desired. Cut an 18-inch (45.7 cm) length of embroidery floss and thread an embroidery needle with three of the strands. Tie an overhand knot at one end.

LAYER two pieces of star-shaped felt. Starting at the midpoint between two points, blanket stitch along the edge of the felt with a ¼-inch (6 mm) seam allowance.

SLIDE a bead onto the needle when you're three stitches from the point. Add another bead and repeat until you reach three stitches past the point. Repeat until only one star point remains.

INSERT a small amount of polyester stuffing into the ornament, using scissors points to push stuffing up and into all areas.

FINISH stitching and adding beads. Stitch into the ornament to hide the floss end between the layers of felt. Trim any excess.

KNOT the end of new floss and stitch through the ornament at one star point. Leaving an 8-inch (20.3 cm) length, stitch back into the ornament and tie the ends together. Trim the excess.

SEW faceted disk beads to the center of each ornament. Attach pre-glued crystals to the front of the ornament with the applicator wand.

SANTA'S TIP: Create your own bead patterns by laying beads in a desirable pattern prior to stitching. The choices are almost limitless.

Glistening Star Garland

A mix of pale pastels, subtle metallic accents, and iridescent beads adds a glistening fairyland touch to any holiday decorating scheme. This garland looks great set against a bold background.

WHAT YOU NEED

25-mm faceted teardrop beads

11° seed beads, pale yellow

20-mm blown glass beads, pale yellow and clear

18-mm round iridescent plastic beads

12-mm round gold plastic beads

8-mm Chinese iridescent crystal beads

4-mm metallized plastic fluted tubes, antique gold

10-mm plastic faceted bicone beads

8-mm glass pearl beads

2° silver-lined iridescent seed beads

6-mm Czech faceted fire-polished glass beads

10-mm frosted resin beads

10-mm faceted plastic beads

3-inch (7.6 cm) head pins

Crimp beads

Flexible .019 beading wire, 9 feet (2.7 m) in length

WHAT YOU DO

THREAD a combination of large and small beads onto the head pins. Leave ¼ inch (6 mm) of each pin free of beads. Bend the end of the pin to form a 90° angle. Use round-nose pliers to form a simple loop.

STRING a crimp bead, 10 seed beads, a teardrop, and 10 additional seed beads onto the wire. Form a loop by running the end of the wire back through the crimp bead. Crimp the bead and carefully trim the excess wire at the short end. Do not snip the long end!

STRING beads onto the wire in a pleasing sequence. When you have covered about 12 inches (30.5 cm), thread six beaded head pins onto the wire. Repeat this sequence until the wire is almost covered.

THREAD a crimp bead, followed by 10 seed beads, a teardrop, and 10 more seed beads to create a loop at the end of the wire. Thread the end of the wire through the crimp bead, pull the wire snugly to make the head pins stand up, and crimp the crimp bead with flat-nosed pliers. Trim the excess wire.

Designed by
ANDREA L. STERN

Heirloom Jewel Ornaments

Back before keepsake ornaments hit the stores, people used to make their own. These jewels are reminiscent of those olden days, when a personal touch meant more than gold.

Gold spray paint

1½-inch (3.8 cm) polystyrene foam ball

16-gauge wire

3-inch (7.6 cm) plumber's chain

Glue

Assortment of plastic and glass beads from old jewelry

New beads such as seed and bugle beads

Sequins in various shapes

Assortment of straight pins

SPRAY paint the ball gold.

FORM a hanger from a 2-inch (5.1 cm) piece of wire, using pliers to make a circular loop at the end of the wire. Thread the plumber's chain onto the loop and close. Dip the bottom of the wire in the glue, then insert it into the top of the ball.

PUT a bead and sequin on a pin, dip it in glue, and insert in the foam ball. Continue using varying sizes of beads until the ball is covered.

SANTA'S TIP: Use a mixture of glass and plastic beads because all glass beads will make the ornament too heavy. If you like, save 2 inches (5.1 cm) from the end of an old necklace to use as a decorative dangler.

Designed by
SHERRI VILOV

Beaded Felt Ornaments

The felt adds color and the beads add sparkle to these stuffed ornaments. Cut the felt into traditional shapes or make something truly unique by letting your imagination run free!

WHAT YOU DO

MAKE patterns from the templates. Cut out the shapes from different colors of felt and attach layers with iron-on adhesive. With invisible thread in the top of the sewing machine and matching thread in the bobbin, zigzag all the way around the adhered pieces of felt.

POSITION the pre-beaded wire on the felt, making shapes as shown. Cut the wire, leaving 1 inch (2.5 cm) at each end without beads. Push the wire through the felt and wind it around using needle-nose pliers. With invisible thread and a beading needle, stitch between the beads every ½ inch (1.3 cm) to hold them in position. Place a dab of glue on the coil of wire on the back.

SEW on other beads with invisible thread.

CUT out the background shapes from the quilt batting. Trim a little smaller than the pattern. Sandwich the quilt batting between the front and the back of the ornament and blanket stitch around the whole edge with matching thread.

PUNCH a hole at the top of the ornament. Open a jump ring with the needle-nose pliers, put one end of the ring through the hole, and then close the jump ring. Run bead-stringing wire through the jump ring. Place a crimp bead over the two ends of the wire and crimp it.

Paved with Beads

These projects do double-duty: use them as glistening package trims or as tree ornaments. Add a note suggesting the gift recipient save the trim as a keepsake ornament.

WHAT YOU NEED

Cookie cutters, preferably with backs, old or new, metal or plastic
Transparent tape (optional)
Metallic gold acrylic paint
Jeweler's glue
Industrial-strength glue
Hot glue gun
Bugle and/or seed beads
Metallic plastic beads
Gold cord
Ribbon

Designed by
SUZIE MILLIONS

WHAT YOU DO

USE cookie cutters with an open handle that you can tie the hanger to. If the cookie cutter handle is inside the cutter, cover the opening with a piece of transparent tape. If the cookie cutter has no back, make a temporary back with transparent tape.

PAINT the back, sides, and front of each cookie cutter with gold paint and let dry.

SQUEEZE jeweler's glue into all the areas of the cutter you want to fill with beads. Holding the cutter over a paper plate, pour beads into all the glued areas. Pat them down into the glue. Let them sit for a minute before turning the cutter upside down to catch the excess. If there are any bare spots, add

more glue and re-bead. Add one bead type at a time until you are satisfied.

ADD larger beads on top using a toothpick to apply a small dot of industrial-strength glue. Press them in place.

MAKE a 4-inch (10.2 cm) loop of gold cord for the hanger. Wrap the ends and tie a knot at the base. Tie the loop to the top of the handle on the back of the cookie cutter, and knot it again twice. Trim the ends to ¼ inch (6 mm).

TIE a piece of ribbon to make a bow. Use a hot glue gun to attach it to the back of the cutter, over the gold cord hanger. Trim the ends if needed.

SANTA'S TIP: Working on paper plates keeps glue off of your work surface, catches the excess beads as you apply them, and allows you to easily funnel beads back into their containers when you're finished.

Greetings &Gifts

Decorating your home for the holidays can be endless fun, but endless trips to crowded malls are not. For this season of giving, these gifts and cards have something you won't find in a store: the special magic of a beautiful object you've made by hand just for its lucky recipient. Show how much you care!

Angels Among Us

An angel celebrates the holidays in style by recycling whenever possible to create art. You can be an angel while making these angelic wings. This project makes two pairs of wings to help spread the joy.

WHAT YOU NEED

Templates (page 127)
Felt
Double-sided iron-on adhesive
Sequins (floral, round, snow-flake, and square)
Seed beads
E-beads
Bugle beads
Beading thread
Matching sewing thread
Ribbon, ⅛ inch (3 mm) wide
20-gauge gold wire

Designed by
TERRY TAYLOR

WHAT YOU DO

COPY the templates. Cut out two pieces of felt from each template using the project photograph as a guide.

ADHERE the iron-on adhesive to the back of each of the smaller pieces. Fuse the smaller piece on top of the larger piece.

STITCH sequins and beads to the smaller pieces as desired, using beading thread. Place the smaller pieces on the wing. Turn the wing over and fuse the shapes together, beads face down. Stitch beads to the lower edge of the wings as desired.

ATTACH the blank wing to the beaded wing using a blanket stitch and sewing thread. Stitch the ribbon in place on the beaded side of the wings in the center.

CUT an 8-inch (20.3 cm) piece of wire and thread on 5 inches (12.7 cm) of beads and sequins. Center the beads and bend the beaded wire into a circle. Twist the ends of the wire together.

Vintage Christmas Cards

A classic Christmas card doesn't have to spend the rest of its life in a drawer. Make a color copy to create a new card! A treasure from the past will someday become a treasure in the future.

WHAT YOU NEED

Vintage Christmas cards
Blank greeting cards
Craft knife
Spray adhesive
All-purpose glue
Glass seed beads or microbeads

Designed by
SKIP WADE

WHAT YOU DO

MAKE a color photocopy of your chosen image from the vintage card. Measure the area to be shown on the blank card. With a straightedge and a craft knife, cut out a window with these dimensions in the front of the card.

TRIM the color copy to frame the chosen image with ¼ inch (6 mm) on all sides.

SPRAY the inside front of the card with spray adhesive. Center the image inside the window. Cut another blank card in half and spray one half with adhesive. Press the glued surfaces together with the color copy between.

PAINT all-purpose glue on the areas of the color copy to receive colored beads (such as the poinsettias in the project photo) using a small paintbrush. Sprinkle the glued areas with seed beads. Once the glue has dried, shake off excess beads.

PAINT all-purpose glue around the edges where the card meets the image. Sprinkle the glued area with seed beads and allow it to dry. Shake off the excess beads.

Hearty Wishes for a very Happy Christmas.

Beaded Gift Tags

Wrapping paper is a must. A ribbon and a bow are nice. To make your gift really special, though, try one of these gift tags. Your recipients will love your present, and they won't forget who sent it.

WHAT YOU NEED

Chipboard
Holly patterned paper
Word patterned paper or ivory cardstock
Decoupage medium
Red stamping ink
Thick craft glue
Memory wire, bracelet size
Green bugle beads
Red bicone beads
Gold tube beads
Green, clear, and gold seed beads
Light green drop bead
Dark green flat round bead
Red round bead
Beige thread
Red, gold, and green sheer ribbon

Designed by
CARLA SCHAUER

WHAT YOU DO

CUT circles 2 ½ inches (6.4 cm) in diameter from the chipboard and holly paper. Decoupage the paper to the chipboard. Ink the edges in red. Cut a phrase from the patterned paper or print it in red on the ivory cardstock. Mount the phrase on the chipboard and ink the edges. Glue it to the chipboard circle.

CUT the memory wire to 3 inches (7.6 cm). Bend the end of the wire with round-nose pliers to form a loop. String the green bugle beads onto the wire, leaving ½ inch (1.3 cm) free. Thread the remaining wire through the loop and twist to secure it. Trim the excess wire. Glue it to the outer edge of the chipboard circle using the craft glue.

CUT a ½-inch (1.3 cm) slit in the top of the chipboard circle. String the beads for the drop using the thread as shown in the project photo.

SLIDE the ends of the thread through the slit and secure on the reverse side. Slide the ribbon through the slit and tie it in a bow.

Bead-Wrapped
Gift
Boxes

When you're giving your craft-loving friend a present in a box,
include beads as both embellishment and part of the gift.

Gift wrap
Jewelry-size gift boxes
Ribbon
Tape
Focal beads
Assorted matching beads
Gold or silver elastic string

WHAT YOU DO

WRAP the gift box. For bow styles, wrap the box with ribbon and tie
a double knot in the center top. Leave the ends hanging until later. For
packages without a bow, tape the ends of the ribbon in place.

THREAD beads onto the elastic string and wrap it around the box. Turn
over the box and tie the ends of the elastic tightly in the center bottom.
Cut off the excess elastic. Place a small piece of tape over the knot.

TIE another double knot in the ribbon to start the bow and hold the
beaded elastic in place. Tie two bows, one on top of the other, with the
ribbon. Cut the ends of the ribbon to length.

Designed by
JOAN K. MORRIS

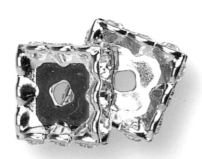

Elegant Velvet Envelopes

Whether you're delivering a plastic gift card or a party invitation, do it in style! These beaded envelopes cushion their contents in plush velvet. Opening one is a treat you must share.

WHAT YOU NEED

Velvet fabric

Satin fabric

Matching thread

Sew-on snap

Wire-wrapped velvet bead trim

Fabric glue

Designed by
CARLA SCHAUER

WHAT YOU DO

PIN the right sides of the velvet and satin together. Cut a rectangle, 11½ x 22 inches (29.2 x 55.9 cm), from the pinned fabric. To form the pointed envelope flap, measure and mark 4 inches (10.2 cm) down each side of the fabric. Measure 5¾ inches (14.6 cm) to the center point across the top. Cut off the corners between the marks.

SEW with right sides together, using ¼-inch (6 mm) seams and leaving a 2½-inch (6.4 cm) hole for turning. Turn the envelope right side out and stitch closed.

FOLD up the envelope pocket, velvet sides together, with the bottom seam reaching ½ inch (1.3 cm) below the flap. Pin the sides together and stitch them up with ¼-inch (6 mm) seams. Turn the envelope velvet side out.

SEW one snap half on the inside point of the envelope. Sew the other snap to the outside of the envelope.

GLUE the velvet beaded trim down the right side of the envelope flap, leaving ½ inch (1.3 cm) of trim on the open end. Fold the trim over 45°, and continue gluing the trim up the left side of the envelope flap. Fold the open trim ends under and glue to secure.

SANTA'S TIP: To make a smaller, jewelry-size envelope, cut the rectangle 5 ½ x 10 inches (14 x 25.4 cm). Measure 2 ¾ inches (7 cm) across the top of the smaller rectangle and 3 inches (7.6 cm) down each side. Cut at the marks to form the envelope flap.

Cards of Christmas Past

Everyone has a blurred, off-kilter, or overexposed photograph of a past Christmas that they lovingly treasure. Share that memory with family or friends in a one-of-a-kind card.

Photograph
Spray adhesive or glue
Blank cards or cardstock
Sequins
Seed beads
Thread

Designed by
TERRY TAYLOR

PHOTOCOPY your photograph on a color copier or scan it into your computer and print out. Cut out your image and adhere it to the card.

OPEN up the card and place it flat on a work surface. Measure the diameter of your sequins. Use a needle to prick holes all around the edge of the photo, slightly less than a sequin's width apart.

THREAD a needle and knot the end. Working from the back, bring the needle up through any pricked hole. Thread on a sequin, followed by a seed bead. Bring the needle back down through the hole and over to an adjacent hole. Keep working around the photo until you have completely covered the edge.

SANTA'S TIP: Don't have any bad or boring photographs? No problem! Search antique stores or online auctions for Christmas photographs. (Yes, people actually toss them out!)

Wrap It Up!

Jars, tubes, bottles, and yes, even boxes. If you love wrapping things for Christmas, then this is the project for you. Wrap it, tag it, and it's ready to go to that special someone.

WHAT YOU NEED

Glass jars with two-part lids
Felt
Felt tree shapes, multiple sizes
Seed beads
Thread
Ribbon
Patterned paper
White eyelets
Cording
Pinking shears
Fabric glue
Hole punch

Designed by
CARLA SCHAUER

WHAT YOU DO

CUT a felt circle ½ inch (1.3 cm) larger than the jar lid with pinking shears. Glue the tree shapes to the center of the circle.

DECORATE the trees with seed beads sewn on with matching thread.

GLUE the felt lid cover to the lid. Trim the excess felt from the lid. Insert it into the ring and twist it onto the jar.

USE pinking shears to cut a strip of felt 1 inch (2.5 cm) wide. Glue a felt tree to the right third of the strip. Bead as described above. Punch holes in each end of the felt strip. Tie the strip onto the jar using ribbon threaded through the holes.

CUT a small tag shape from felt. Glue a small tree to the bottom right corner. Bead the tree. Glue the tag to the patterned paper and cut the tag slightly larger than the felt. Punch a hole in the top of the tag and set an eyelet in the hole. Tie to the lid ring with cording.

Jewel Trimmed Gift Bags

If holiday gift-wrapping is *not* your cup of tea, then this project can save you. These gift bags are easy to make and perfect for any small gift. They're truly the gift that keeps on regifting.

WHAT YOU NEED

Bead trim ribbon
Store-bought or handmade gift bags
Matching thread

Designed by
SKIP WADE

WHAT YOU DO

CUT the ribbon into pieces long enough to circle the top of the gift bag or run down the side of the bag. If you have enough ribbon, do both!

HAND stitch (or machine stitch) the ribbon to the top and side of the gift bag, as desired.

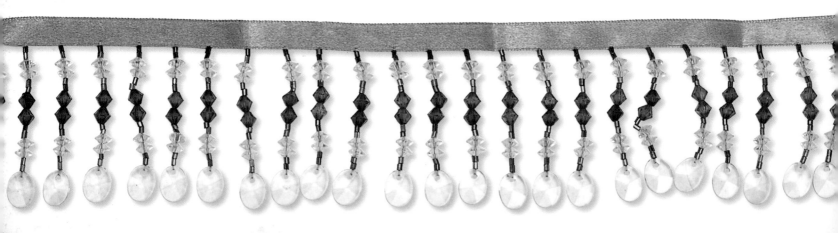

Silver Snowflake Greetings

Even if you live in Hawaii, snow and snowflakes are inextricably linked to the Christmas season. Now you can make and send holiday cards that evoke that same spirit. No two are exactly alike!

Designed by
TERRY TAYLOR

WHAT YOU NEED

Jar lid or other small circular object
Cards and matching envelopes
Silver embroidery floss
Snowflake beads or sequins
Seed beads
Tape
Craft glue

WHAT YOU DO

TRACE the jar lid onto scrap paper. Cut it out and fold the circle in half. Fold the half circle into thirds. Unfold the circle and place it on a card. Mark the six evenly spaced points on the card. Open the card and pierce each mark with a needle.

THREAD a needle with two 18-inch (45.7 cm) strands of silver floss. Thread the needle up through the back of the card. Pull the thread almost all the way through and then secure the end with tape. Pass the needle down into the opposite hole. Bring the needle back up through an adjacent hole and down through the opposite hole. Continue until you have three stitched lines.

BRING the needle up through an adjacent hole. String a snowflake and a seed bead. Bring the needle back down through the same hole, securing the beads. Work around the circle. Finish by taping the thread end to the card's back.

HIDE the stitching on the back by cutting out a piece of matching cardstock or decorative paper slightly larger than your circle. Glue it in place.

SANTA'S TIP: These plastic snowflakes were purchased to be used as beads, but turned out to have no holes in them. No problem: anything can become a bead if you drill a hole in it!

The Christmas Beading Workshop

No doubt you're as busy as an elf this time of year: shopping, cooking, decorating, and crafting in preparation for the holidays. Before you add a beading project to your list, take a tip from Santa's helpers and get your workshop in order for maximum merriment and productivity. With the right materials, tools, and techniques, your Christmas craft wishes are sure to come true.

"STOCKING" UP ON BEADS

If the beading bug bit you long ago, chances are you've already got quite a collection. But you've been oh so good this year—why not treat yourself to a trip to the bead store?

Choosing beads for your Christmas project is bound to get you in the holiday spirit. There are so many kinds to chose from, each offering color, texture, glimmer, shimmer, and shine! Christmas is no time to hold back. Be bold in your choices and in your designs—there's no such thing as over the top! Use this guide to help you make your bead-shopping list and check it twice before heading out into the holiday crowds.

SEED BEADS

Seed beads come in several different sizes, each assigned a number from 1 to 15. The number roughly describes the number of beads that can be strung per inch. Remember this rule of thumb: the larger the number, the smaller the bead. Seed beads are great for bead stitching projects (see page 122), but they can be used in many other ways, too: as spacers, paired with sequins, or stitched to felt beads to add texture. Silver-, copper-, and bronze-lined seed beads might be a perfect choice for a holiday project, and those with a luster or AB (aurora borealis) finish will make your Christmas lights dance.

CRYSTAL AND GLASS BEADS

In the sparkliest of seasons, crystal and glass beads capture and reflect your candle and Christmas lights, creating that twinkle that makes the season brighter. While you may want to use the more expensive crystals sparingly, you can find affordable alternatives. Faceted Czech glass-fired beads or cubic zirconia beads give you the glitter for less green.

HANDMADE LAMPWORK BEADS

Made from melted glass rods, lampwork beads are highly decorative and are often used as focal point beads. Look for special holiday selections—snowmen, Christmas trees, perhaps a red-nosed reindeer?

PRESTRUNG BEADED FRINGE AND GARLAND

Using prestrung beaded fringe or garland offers you a little convenience and a little more time to get your holiday errands done. In the months leading up to the holidays, you'll find a variety of garlands, strands, and fringes at craft stores, and they're becoming more and more affordable.

FIBER OR FELT BEADS

As warm and fuzzy as a Christmas stocking, felt beads are a perfect choice for holiday projects. It's easy to create a hole in felt beads if the ones you find don't have them. Felt beads add a whimsical touch and can even be embellished with tiny seed beads.

MERCURY AND GLASS BEADS

Old mercury glass ornaments are among the most iconic symbols of Christmas. The glass, also called Lauscha glass after the city in Germany where they were first manufactured, was also made into beads that were used in garlands and other Christmas decorations. You can find mercury glass beads in antique stores or online auctions. Incorporate the garland into a project, or carefully unstring it and use the beads for your own creation.

PONY BEADS

Pony beads are often the first type of beads kids learn to work with. Round with a large hole, they're easy to work with, easy to find, and inexpensive to buy.

MICROBEADS

The tiniest of beads can make for the merriest of Christmas crafts. Tiny, hole-less beads that have become a favorite of paper crafters, microbeads are a kind of glitter/seed bead hybrid that offers interesting effects. With their three-dimensional texture, they can be made to resemble a layer of new-fallen snow or the petals of a poinsettia. If you're not confident with your bead stitching and stringing skills, micro-beads may be the answer—they're applied with glue.

SEQUINS

Purists might scoff at even putting them in the same category with crystal and lampwork beads. But they've got holes, and they sparkle, so at this time of year, why quibble? On ornaments, stockings, and even Christmas sweaters, sequins have long been a staple of holiday decorating. Iridescent or metallic, flat or textured, round or snowflake-shaped—there's a tantalizing variety to choose from. You can pin them into foam to make wreaths, sew them onto fabric runners, or stitch them onto paper cards. Layer them with beads pinned on top or string them onto a garland.

BEADS OF CHRISTMAS PAST

Vintage beads—in whatever shape, color, or size you can find them—can add that perfect touch of nostalgia to your Christmas project. Do you have some old necklaces, brooches, or earrings around that you never use? They could happily find a home in a Christmas project that you'll look forward to unpacking and displaying each year.

MAKE-IT-YOURSELF-BEADS

It's the right size, but there's no hole. Is it a bead? Not yet! A drill and a small drill bit can help you turn that foam, wood, or clay ball into a bead. You can make beads from paper, dough, or wood. Just put on some Christmas tunes and protective goggles, pour yourself a glass of eggnog, and power up the drill!

Jingle bells can become beads, too. With a little maneuvering you can thread wire through the openings without restricting its musical quality. Some packaged bells (found in craft stores) even come with hooks on top, making them even easier to string together.

BEAD FINDINGS

To put your projects together—and keep them together for Christmases to come—you may need a few of those metal pieces that jewelry makers call findings.

Crimp beads are small beads or tubes used in place of knots to keep beads in place. Crimp beads are useful when your wire is thin and doesn't hold knots well, or you want your wire to have a smooth appearance. Simply slide crimp beads onto the wire and "crimp" flat with needle-nose pliers.

Jump rings are a mainstay of jewelry designers, but you might find they come in handy for your Christmas projects, too. You can use them for strings or strands that need to be hung, or for that special bead that needs to dangle down a little further than the others.

SANTA'S SUPPLY SACK: YOUR MATERIALS WISH LIST

Picking your beads is the artistic part. But even Santa's elves know that there's a practical side to creating all those Christmas goodies. With the right materials and tools at your side, you'll be ready for Christmas morning.

Most of what you need to know about beading materials is common sense. You need a stronger material to attach a heavier bead. You need a fray-resistant material to get through small holes in small beads. You need the right kind of glue to keep porous material together. Strength, durability, and flexibility—keep these factors in mind and you're sure to create the holly, jolly projects that your friends and family will be talking about for many Christmases to come.

WIRE

Wire is sold in a variety of gauges: the smaller the gauge, the thicker the wire. For example, a 14-gauge wire is thicker than a 24-gauge wire. Aside from the gauge, you'll also find wire sold in different types of "hardness," from dead-soft to half-hard to full-hard. Dead-soft, for example, can be worked by hand, while full-hard requires tools to bend. For the projects in this book, you'll work with one of the following types of wire

NYLON-COATED BEADING WIRE

You can find this flexible beading wire in many different lengths and widths, and even in different colors (red and green perhaps?). Although it's strong and flexible, it doesn't hold knots well, so it's better used with crimp beads or tubes if you want your beads to stay in place. It has a "drapey" quality, making it a good choice if you have heavy beads that you'd like to have dangle or a poor choice if you'd like your beads to stay taut and close together. It's also great for wrapping around strong, durable structures or surfaces, such as wreath forms or even heavier wire.

COPPER OR BRASS CRAFT WIRE

While it's strong and can retain its shape, it's flexible enough for wrapping, twisting, and weaving, and can often be worked by hand. Although the core is copper, you can find it in many different colors.

SILVER OR SILVER-PLATE WIRE

Both of these types of wire are soft and pliable, but as you might guess, the sterling silver wire is more expensive. Silver-plate wire has a copper core, so it's a more affordable alternative to sterling silver wire. Either type is stunning with icy-cool blue or clear crystal beads for the holidays.

THREAD

When it comes to sewing beads onto projects, or stringing them together, you'll want to look for one of the following in your local sewing or craft store.

BEADING THREAD

If you'll be stitching with beads, you'll need this thin nylon thread that comes in single or double strands, waxed or unwaxed. Choose a color that disappears into or stands out from the material you're stitching into, depending upon the effect you're trying to achieve. Use beading thread with a beading needle.

SEWING THREAD

You can use regular sewing thread for bead embroidery projects, with a few caveats. First, your thread will obviously need to be strong enough to support the weight of the beads (the more lightweight, the better). You'll also need to condition the thread with beeswax or thread conditioner to keep it from fraying. And lastly, you'll need to make sure your sewing needle will fit through the hole in your bead.

WAXED LINEN THREAD

Waxed linen thread holds knots well, so it's a great choice for bead stringing projects. The catch? It's a bit thicker than some beading thread, so you'll need to use it with beads that have larger holes

GLUE

Jewelry glue is a specialty glue (found in craft stores) that bonds nonporous and semiporous materials. You can use it with glass or plastic beads, wire, or other kinds of metals. It dries clear and strong and provides a permanent bond.

Craft glue can be used for some types of beads on some types of materials.

You can use it to adhere beads to felt, for example, but you'll need to be careful (see page 123 for some tips). You can glue microbeads to paper with regular craft glue as well. If you use regular craft glue on polystyrene foam, you need to brush it on lightly, because it will not dry properly when it's poured on. Always select the clear-drying variety.

If you'll be bonding beads to fabric, *fabric glue* generally provides a stronger bond than craft glue, although it can depend on the type of bead you're using.

OTHER GOODIES

If you use your imagination, the list of materials you can incorporate into your beaded projects is pretty much endless. Here are just a few more items you can look for to spark your creativity.

FELT

There's something about this warm, fuzzy fabric that just says "Christmas craft." Buy it in red and green and embellish it with sequins. Glue it to a Christmas tree form for an instant accessory.

PATTERNED PAPERS

Even if you don't make handmade cards any other time of the year, Christmas is your chance to make an impression. Use any of the myriad patterned scrapbook papers or handmade papers available at your local craft or art supply store. Add sequins, beads, glitter, or microbeads for texture, gluing or stitching them in place.

PURCHASED HOME ACCENTS

A plain white lampshade, an ordinary red table runner—they're just calling out for some Christmas cheer! Bead them up with fringe, stitched sequins, or glued-on glitter. Solid-color felt stockings, a simple Christmas tree skirt—you don't have to sew them yourself, just add your creative touch to them while saving a little extra time for other holiday pleasures.

POLYSTYRENE FOAM FORMS

Round for ornament, cone-shaped for Christmas trees—you can even get them shaped like bells, sleds, or reindeer. Cover the surface with sequins or microbeads; add ribbon, felt, or any other kind of fabric. Polystyrene foam forms are the perfect building blocks for your beaded Christmas crafts.

TOOLS YULE USE

You wouldn't try making reindeer-shaped cookies without your trusty Rudolph cookie cutter. Don't tackle your Christmas beading project without the right tools on hand either.

BEADING NEEDLES

Used for sewing or embroidering with beads, beading needles are very long, thin, and flexible needles designed to use with beading thread (see page 116). You can hold several beads at a time. You can find them in most craft or bead stores. Beading needles come in different sizes from 10 to 15, with 10 being the thinnest and 15 being the thickest.

SEWING, EMBROIDERY, OR MILLINERY NEEDLES

You can use sewing needles for bead sewing and embroidery projects, provided they'll pass through the holes in your beads. If you can find them, milliner's needles might be a better choice—they're longer and more flexible than sewing needles.

BIG EYE NEEDLES

These needles, very useful for bead weaving and beading projects that require a change of thread, have an eye that runs down the entire shaft of the needle. They're easy to thread and can fit through even the tiniest of beads.

STRAIGHT PINS AND TACKS

Straight pins are great for adding sequins to permeable surfaces such as polystyrene foam. You can get them in a variety of lengths, and even with decorative pearl or glass heads—giving them the appearance of a bead.

PLIERS

You'll find two types of pliers invaluable for your beading projects. *Round-nose pliers* are versatile tools with rounded "jaws" that taper toward the ends to create loops in wire. Flat on the inside of the jaw and rounded on the exterior, *needle-nose pliers* are good for grasping and bending wire or getting inside small loops.

WIRE CUTTERS

It's always good to have a set of these on hand when you're working with wire. They're more effective than scissors or pliers for cutting wire (although you could try either of those tools in a pinch). Jewelers' wire cutters have a narrow, sharp point that can get inside tiny loops, while heavy-duty wire cutters are used for thick-gauge wires.

TWEEZERS

For picking up and positioning tiny beads, tweezers can really come in handy. You can use them to place individual beads on glued surfaces, or to pull through thread or wire knots and loops when your pliers are too big. If you're using sewing thread or linen thread, you may even be able to use them to undo a knot gone wrong.

Often used in jewelry making when small, tight knots are needed, *beading tweezers* have a specialized tip that can get a good grip on tiny beads or get in between the strands of a knot.

GLUE GUN AND GLUE STICKS

This tool is a great alternative to sewing when your Christmas craft time is limited. You can hot glue beaded fringe to fabric, or use it to attach beads to any other nonporous surface, but it's not the best for heirloom-quality projects because it will eventually crack and start to yellow.

You've got almost everything you need to start decking the halls with your beaded projects, but you'll need a little know-how to do it right. Use some of these tried and true techniques and you'll be beading around the Christmas tree in no time.

SEASON'S BEADINGS:
A HO-HO HOW-TO

HARK! THE HERALD ANGELS STRING

Stringing a cranberry and popcorn garland to hang on the tree is a classic Christmas pastime. Stringing beads is just as much fun and might be even easier. While cranberry-popcorn garlands start with a needle and thread, you may use wire, beading thread, or other materials (see page 115) for bead stringing.

Arrange your beads in advance so you know your focal point bead (if you have one) will appear in the middle. Start with a knot or crimp bead on one end of your string or thread. Add your beads, using a crimp bead or knot after certain beads if you want them to stand out from the others. End your strand with another crimp bead or a knot.

KNOTTY IS NICE

If your project involves stringing and you want your beads to stay in place, you'll need to knot. There are several different ways to do it.

An *overhand knot* (figure 1) is useful for securing beads. Just take one side of the thread and cross it over the other to form a loop, then pull the free end of the thread through the loop.

figure 1

figure 2

A *square knot* (figure 2) is another strong hold. To make it, position one end of the thread over the other to form a loop, then pull the thread through the loop. Pass it around the loop again and pull tightly (it's essentially like making two overhand knots).

figure 3

A *lark's head knot* (figure 3) is a simple knot, perfect for a zipper pull or fringe. Fold the thread in half and run the folded point through a loop, a wire, a zipper, or whatever you want to connect to. Then tuck both ends through the fold and pull tight.

You may also add a dot of glue or clear nail polish over your knot to make sure it doesn't unravel. Apply it with a toothpick for best results (see page 123).

If you want to hide your knot under a bead, leave a tail of thread as you're stringing. When you come to the place where you need a knot, thread the tail onto another needle and push it through the bead or beads. When you come out of the bead, loop the loose thread around the main thread and put the second needle through the loop twice, creating a knot. Pull it tight and then sew through the next bead. The knot should pull into the next bead and be hidden by it.

WIRE TIPS FROM THE ELVES

Making wire loops and wraps in your projects will keep them permanently together. It also gives you a chance to match accents of shiny silver or gold (or copper if you like) with your colorful array of beads.

SIMPLE LOOP

Loops are often used at the end of a wire to keep beads from falling off. Just follow the steps shown in figure 4. First, use pliers to bend your wire at a 90° angle (the short end of the wire should be long enough to create the size loop you want). Hold the tip of the short end in the jaws of a pair of round-nose pliers and begin to bend it back gradually into a circle (you will probably have to shift the position of the pliers several times for a uniform curve). You're done when the loop almost touches the base.

figure 4

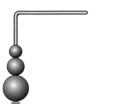

figure 5

WRAPPED LOOP

A wrapped loop starts out like a simple loop, but the short end of the wire should be long enough to wrap back around the long end of the wire. With each wrap, the wire should touch the previous wrap to give the appearance of a coil (figure 5).

SIMPLE TWIST

To make a twist, cross the ends of the wire, then start wrapping one end back around the base (if your wire is thick, you'll need pliers to do this).

MRS. CLAUS' STITCHING TIPS

Bead embroidery is just another way of saying "sewing with beads." When embroidering with beads, it's important to keep in mind the weight and size of your beads in relation to the weight of your fabric. A lightweight fabric could support a few lightweight beads, but if you start adding too many, it may sag. A heavier fabric can support more beads or heavier beads, but might be more difficult to sew through or might not have the drape you're looking for. Experiment a little first before committing to a certain combination of fabric and beads.

Backstitch is used most commonly for a strong and secure bond between bead and fabric. Make an overhand knot (see page 120) at the end of your thread. Sew up from the wrong side of the fabric to the right side, and then add your bead or beads (typically no more than three at a time) sewing through the bead holes and then holding the beads against the fabric. Sew back down into the fabric snug against the last bead on your thread and come back up through to the right side. Sew through the last couple of beads again, and then back down into the fabric. Come back up through to the right side, add more beads, and repeat the process.

Couching is another method used for a secure bond. Because it's a bit time-consuming, it's best for projects using a smaller number of beads. Make a knot at the end of your thread and bring the needle up from wrong side to right side. Add the beads and lay them down on the fabric, then go back through to the wrong side. Come back up and make a stitch between each bead (this can be done with the needle and thread you're already using, or a separate set).

You can use a *running stitch* for a simple, but less secure, bond with the fabric. Start from the wrong side of the fabric and come up through the right side. Thread a few beads onto your needle and thread, and then stitch back into the fabric. Come back up and make a small stitch in front of the last bead you added (going back down into the fabric), then come back up and add more beads. Repeat the process to make a continuous line of beads on your fabric.

If you just want to add one bead or sequin at a time in various places (as opposed to a line of beads), you can use the *spot stitch.* Start from the wrong side of the fabric, sew up to the right side, and add your bead or sequin. Sew back into the fabric and come up in the spot where you want to place the next bead and repeat the process. If you'll only be adding one bead, knot off the thread on the wrong side of the fabric once you've added the first bead. You can always go back through the bead one more time for a more secure hold if you wish.

AVOID A GLUE CHRISTMAS!

Beads and glue—sounds like a big mess, doesn't it? It can be if you're not careful. If you're going to be covering a large area with glue, use a brush or other spreader to do the work for you. Use tweezers to lay the beads down on the surface—this will give you more control and make sure that glue doesn't get onto the bead surface that will be facing outward.

Toothpicks are another great tool to have on hand when you're beading with glue. Use them for applying small dabs of glue onto your surface. You can also "thread" a toothpick with beads (if they're large enough) and drop them into place one by one.

Wax paper can come in handy for beading a large surface as well. You can cover a rounded object (such as an ornament) with beads by placing it on the wax paper and brushing it with glue, then sprinkling beads on top and rolling the object around on top of the wax paper. Any places that don't get covered can be filled in with more sprinkling or by placing beads with a toothpick or tweezers.

For thin lines of beads on fabric or another nonporous surface, use glue straight from the bottle, testing on a piece of scrap material first to make sure you have the consistency you want before applying the glue to your project. This will help you avoid lumps, clumps, and splurts that can be hard to remove.

Templates and Patterns

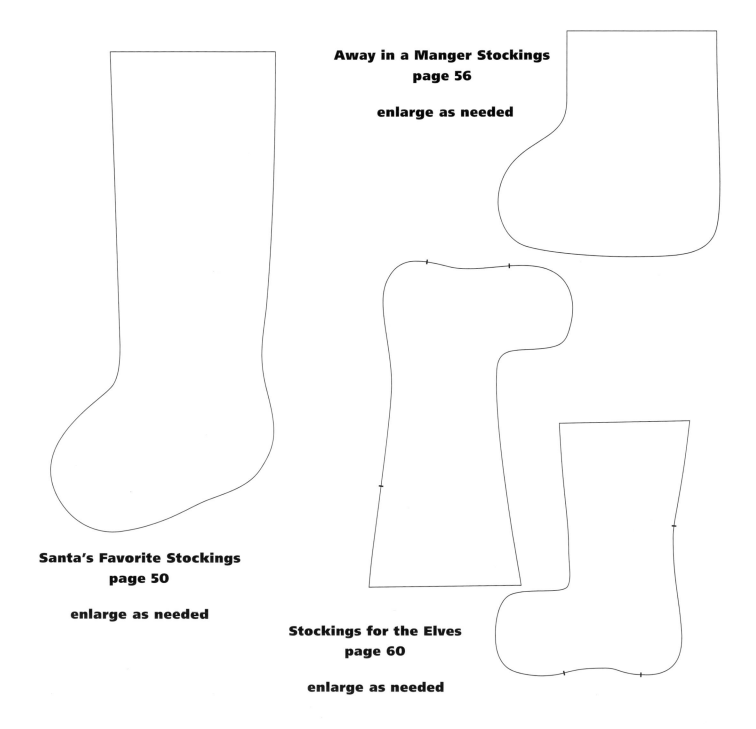

Away in a Manger Stockings
page 56

enlarge as needed

Santa's Favorite Stockings
page 50

enlarge as needed

Stockings for the Elves
page 60

enlarge as needed

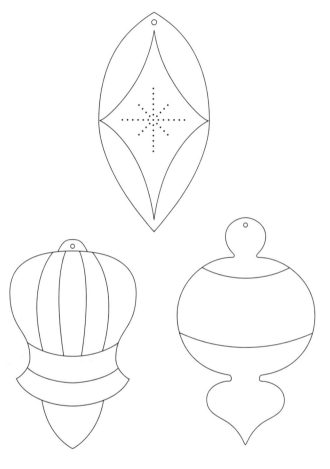

Away in a Manger Stockings
page 56

Berry Beaded Coasters (leaf only)
page 16

enlarge as needed

Beaded Felt Ornaments
page 86

enlarge as needed

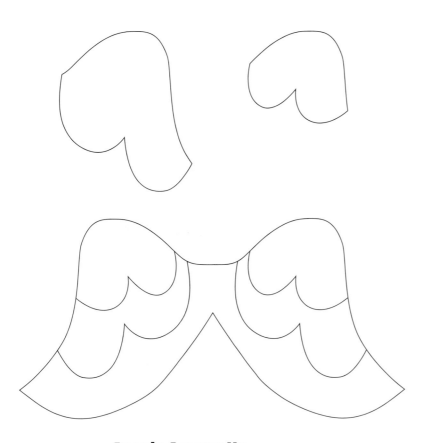

Angels Among Us
page 92

enlarge as needed

Away in a Manger Stockings (cuff)
page 56

enlarge as needed

About the Designers

MELONY BRADLEY is a full-time creative designer specializing in beaded crafts, recycled crafts, and kids projects. It's all about crafts for Melony; when she's *not* working on project design, she writes technique articles for the craft industry. A member of the Craft and Hobby Association (CHA), she demonstrates at trade shows and teaches classes. She's been published in numerous magazines.

CANDIE COOPER started making jewelry in high school and hasn't stopped since. Her passion lies in designing jewelry from unique materials in vibrant colors. She's the author of *Felted Jewelry* and the co-author of *Designer Needle Felting* (both from Lark Books). Her jewelry has been exhibited throughout the United States, England, and Europe. See more of her work on her website at www.candiecooper.com.

GEORGIE ANNE JAGGERS is a beaded jewelry and home accents artist living in Asheville, North Carolina. By day she manages a bead store—Chevron Trading Post & Bead Company—and by night she's a dance instructor. She draws her inspiration from the beauty of the mountains that surround her. She has taught the art of beading for over six years, and she's been featured in magazines, books, and television shows.

LORINE MASON is a multimedia artist in love with crafting. She shares her skills and creativity with others every chance she gets. Designing, along with a busy teaching schedule, provides her the perfect outlet for her creative energy. You can find her work in numerous magazines, books, and project sheets. Lorine lives with her husband and two daughters in Herndon, Virginia.

SUZIE MILLIONS is an artist, compulsive collector, and author of *The Complete Book of Retro Crafts* (Lark Books). Her paintings and shrines (her home has a walk-in Hank Williams shrine) are shown and collected extensively. Suzie and her musician/artist/compulsive collector husband live in an overstuffed cabin in the Western North Carolina woods. To learn more, visit her website at www.suziemillions.com.

JOAN K. MORRIS has a colorful and artistic past that includes creative swings through such diverse careers as ceramics and costume design for motion pictures. Joan has contributed projects for numerous Lark Books publications, including, *Extreme Office Crafts, Cutting-Edge Decoupage, Pretty Little Pincushions, Button! Button!, Pretty Little Potholders, 50 Nifty Beaded Cards*, and many more.

SONYA NIMRI loves turning over-looked items into sought-after treasures, drinking Mariage Frères tea, pruning her lavender, and beading everything in her house. She is the author of *Just for the Frill of It* and *Beadalicious* (both from Watson-Guptill). She's contributed to the *Los Angeles Times* and *Craft: Magazine*, and she's appeared on HGTV and the Today show. She maintains a DIY website at www.sonyastyle.com.

CARLA SCHAUER began scrapbooking shortly after the birth of her first child. The craft quickly broadened her interests to stamping, card making, and other paper arts. As a freelance designer, her work has been featured in a variety of paper crafting books and magazines. Carla resides in Ohio with her husband, two sons, and daughter, who fill her days with laughter while providing numerous scrapbooking subjects.

ANDREA L. STERN grew up surrounded by a family who all made some type of art, so it was inevitable that she would become an artist herself. From drawings, she progressed to painting, beadwork, and quilting. She received a degree in art history and put it to use when she owned her own bead business. See examples of her work at www.embellishmentcafe.com and on her blog at andibeads.blogspot.com.

SHERRI VILOV works as a visual merchandiser while trying to decide what she wants to do when she grows up. She's dabbled in everything from sewing to welding, including such arts and crafts as jewelry design, mosaics, papermaking, bookbinding, and collage. In her spare time, she takes art classes and haunts thrift stores or yard sales, finding other people's junk to creatively recycle into treasures. Find her work at her online store Funky Junk at slvilov.etsy.com.

SKIP WADE is a freelance stylist/designer in Asheville, North Carolina, who works with fashion, furniture, domestics, and photography. "The only thing I don't do is write," he says. His work has appeared in a number of Lark Books publications, including *Decorating Your First Apartment, Decorating with Mini-Lights, Fun & Fabulous Curtains to Sew, The Beaded Home*, and *Button! Button!*

LINDA WILLIS is a self-taught quilter, doll maker, mixed media artist, gardener, and chef. She teaches classes at a local fabric shop and beyond. Presently working for Allison and Tracy Stilwell of Artgirlz, Linda enjoys making art on her own and traveling the country. Her guiding philosophies are: "What if," "Why not," and "Whatever blows your dress up." She lives, works, and plays mainly in Rhode Island.

About
the
Author

TERRY TAYLOR is a senior editor at Lark Books, but he's also an accomplished jewelry designer. Known affectionately as the Curmudgeonly Crafter for his monthly column in Lark Books' online newsletter (see www.larkbooks.com/article/newsletters), he's also authored quite a few books including *Altered Art, Artful Paper Dolls*, and *The Artful Storybook* (and lots more titles, believe it or not). In addition to his other passions, he has a collection of vintage Santa Claus figures, Santa boots, and Christmas postcards that he digs out when the spirit moves him.

It's all on www.larkbooks.com

Can't find the materials you need to create a project? Search our database for craft suppliers & sources for hard-to-find materials.

Got an idea for a book? Read our book proposal guidelines and contact us.

Want to show off your work? Browse current calls for entries.

Want to know what new and exciting books we're working on? Sign up for our free e-newsletter.

Feeling crafty? Find free, downloadable project directions on the site.

Interested in learning more about the authors, designers & editors who create Lark books?

Index